Celebrations around the World

Level 9 – Gold

Helpful Hints for Reading at Home

The graphemes (written letters) and phonemes (units of sound) used throughout this series are aligned with Letters and Sounds. This offers a consistent approach to learning whether reading at home or in the classroom.

HERE ARE SOME COMMON WORDS THAT YOUR CHILD MIGHT FIND TRICKY:

water	where	would	know	thought	through	couldn't
laughed	eyes	once	we're	school	can't	our

TOP TIPS FOR HELPING YOUR CHILD TO READ:

- Encourage your child to read aloud as well as silently to themselves.
- Allow your child time to absorb the text and make comments.
- Ask simple questions about the text to assess understanding.
- Encourage your child to clarify the meaning of new vocabulary.

This book focuses on developing independence, fluency and comprehension. It is a Gold level 9 book band.

©This edition published 2025. First published in 2023.
BookLife Publishing Ltd.
King's Lynn, Norfolk PE30 4LS, UK

ISBN 978-1-80505-057-5

All rights reserved. Printed in India.
A catalogue record for this book is available from the British Library.

Celebrations around the World
Written by Joanna Brundle
Adapted by Rebecca Phillips-Bartlett
Designed by Isabella Croker

Image Credits Images are courtesy of Shutterstock.com. With thanks to Getty Images, Thinkstock Photo and iStockphoto. Cover – Carlos Ivan Palacios, Marish, Yuganov Konstantin. p4–5 – IVASHstudio, rozbyshaka. p6–7 – MIA Studio, Teo Wei Keong. p8–9 – Cait Eire, pics721. p10–11 – Drazen Zigic, niranana. p12–13 – SMDSS, StockImageFactory.com. p14–15 – AGCuesta, Hugo Brizard – YouGoPhoto. p16–17 – digidreamgrafix, LightField Studios. p18–19 – blueeyes, Golden Pixels LLC. p20–21 – Inara Prusakova, Rimma Bondarenko.

Contents

Page 4   What Are Celebrations?

Page 6   Chinese New Year

Page 8   St Patrick's Day

Page 10   Ramadan

Page 12   Diwali

Page 14   Day of the Dead

Page 16   Thanksgiving

Page 18   Hanukkah

Page 20   Christmas

Page 22   Index

Page 23   Questions

What Are Celebrations?

Celebrations are times when people come together to mark special events. There are many different types of celebrations. Some celebrations can be part of a person's religion, a country's history, or part of family life.

People use celebrations to give thanks and show what is important to them and their culture. For some celebrations, people might have certain customs, eat certain foods, wear special clothes or listen to a certain type of music.

Chinese New Year

Chinese New Year or Lunar New Year is celebrated by Chinese people all over the world. The celebrations often last many weeks. On Lunar New Year's Eve, children are given money in red envelopes as a gift.

Families often celebrate Lunar New Year with a big meal and by staying up very late. On New Year's Day they celebrate with fireworks and parades. The parades often include fancy dress, dancing, acrobatics and drums.

St Patrick's Day

Some countries have national days named after saints. Saints are people who are believed to be very good. Saint Patrick is the patron saint of Ireland, so on the 17th of March people in Ireland celebrate St Patrick's Day.

St Patrick's Day is now celebrated in many countries across the world. Other countries use this day to celebrate Ireland. St Patrick's Day is celebrated with parades.

The Chicago River in the USA is dyed green for St Patrick's Day.

Ramadan

Ramadan is a very important month for Muslims all over the world. During Ramadan, Muslims do not eat anything during daylight hours. This is called a fast. Once the sun sets, families meet to eat big meals together.

Muslims use the month of Ramadan to focus on their religion, Islam. It helps them feel closer to their religion and their loved ones. Many Muslims also raise money or donate supplies to other people during Ramadan.

Diwali

Diwali is a five-day celebration also known as the Festival of Lights. It is celebrated by Hindus, Jains and Sikhs all over the world. The Diwali story is different in different places, but it always celebrates good winning over evil.

During Diwali people light small oil lamps. These lamps are used to invite the goddess of good fortune, called Lakshmi, into their homes. People also use colourful powder or sand to make patterns called rangoli.

Rangoli

Day of the Dead

Day of the Dead is a festival that takes place every year in Mexico and other countries including Spain and Brazil. This festival celebrates the lives of people who have died. People use it to remember their loved ones.

People set up small alters called ofrendas in their homes. These alters are decorated with photographs, candles, marigolds and sugar skulls. During the festival, people often dress up and wear skull masks or makeup.

Thanksgiving

On the third Thursday of November, many Americans celebrate Thanksgiving. On Thanksgiving, people gather with their families and celebrate with a meal. Many families use this time to think about the things for which they are grateful.

As well as spending time together, many families also use Thanksgiving to help other people by volunteering or donating food. Thanksgiving is often celebrated with a big parade which includes marching bands, floats and musical performances.

Hanukkah

Hanukkah is a religious festival celebrated by Jewish people. The festival celebrates a miracle that happened long ago. A lamp that only had enough oil to last one day managed to stay alight for eight days. Therefore, Hanukkah lasts eight days.

During Hanukkah, Jewish people celebrate using a candlestick called a menorah. The menorah has nine candles. Each evening of Hanukkah a different candle is lit. There is one candle for every day that the lamp from the miracle burnt.

Christmas

Christmas is celebrated in many ways in different places. In the UK, people give presents and eat Christmas dinner on the 25th of December. In other countries, including Norway, Denmark and Sweden, these things happen on the 24th of December.

Many different foods are eaten around the world at Christmas. In Denmark, they eat rice pudding with a whole almond hidden inside. Whoever finds the almond gets a gift.

In Italy, people bake a type of bread called a panettone.

Index

candles 15, 19
family 4, 7, 10, 16–17
festivals 12, 14–15, 18
parades 7, 9, 17
religion 4, 11, 18

How to Use an Index

An index helps us to find information in a book. Each word has a set of page numbers. These page numbers are where you can find information about that word.

Page numbers

Example: balloons 5, 8–10, 19

Important word

This means page 8, page 10, and all the pages in between. Here, it means pages 8, 9 and 10.

Questions

1. What are some different types of celebrations?

2. Which religion celebrates Ramadan?

3. In Norway, when do families open their Christmas presents?

4. Use the contents page to find out about St Patrick's Day.

5. Use the index page to find candles in this book.